The Ultimate Zebra Book for Kids

100+ Amazing Zebra Facts, Photos, Quiz & More

Jenny Kellett

BELLANOVA
MELBOURNE · SOFIA · BERLIN

Copyright © 2026 by Jenny Kellett

Zebras: The Ultimate Zebra Book
www.bellanovabooks.com

ISBN: 978-619-7695-37-3
Imprint: Bellanova Books

All rights reserved. No part of this book may be reproduced in any form by any electronic or mechanical means including photocopying, recording, or information storage and retrieval without permission in writing from the author.

Contents

Introduction 4
Zebras - The Basics 7
Characteristics 14
Their Daily Lives 26
Subspecies of Zebras 43
   Grévy's Zebra 44
   Plains Zebra 46
   Mountain Zebra 48
From Birth to Adulthood 52
Zebras and Humans 64
Zebras: Conservation 74
Zebra Quiz 76
  Answers 80
Word search 82
Sources 85

Introduction

The zebra's beautiful, bold stripes make them one of the most recognisable animals in the world. A favourite for zoo and safari visitors, zebras are much more than just horses with stripes! This book takes a closer look at one of Africa's most beautiful animals and you will learn more about their behaviours, characteristics, and the problems they face.

At the end, you can test your new knowledge in our zebra quiz! Are you ready? *Let's go!*

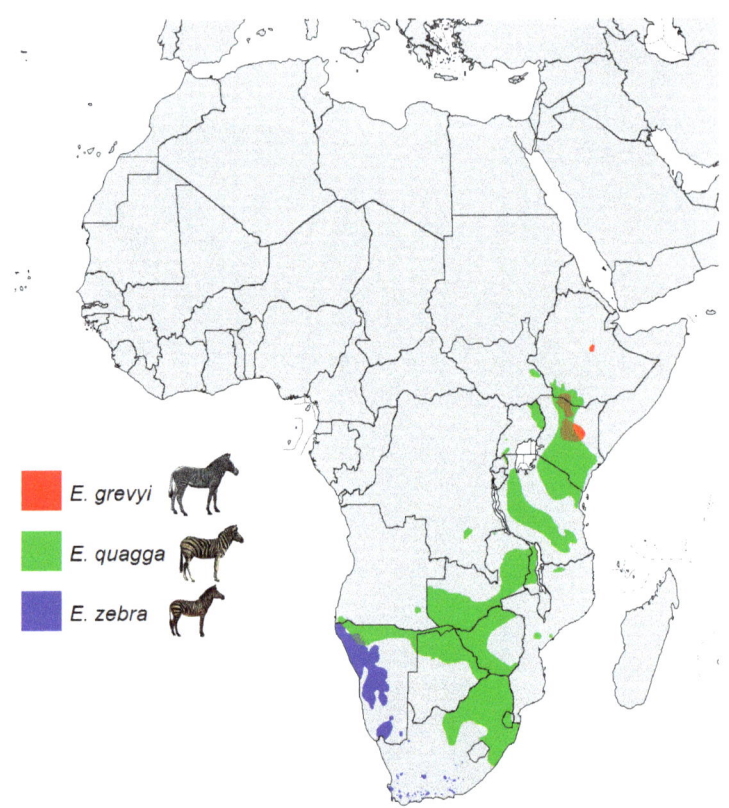

Range of zebra species. *Credit: Mario Massone*

ZEBRAS: THE BASICS

What are zebras and where do they live?

Zebras live in eastern and southern Africa. Their habitats are very diverse and include savannas, shrublands, woodlands, grasslands, and mountainous areas.

• • •

Zebras are in the same family (*Equus*) as horses and asses. However, unlike their close friends, zebras have never been properly domesticated.

Around 2.8 million years ago, zebras and asses were the same animals. At this time, zebras started to evolve into what they are today—with the three separate species forming around one million years later.

•••

The ancient Greeks and Romans called the zebra *hippotigris*, meaning 'horse tiger'.

•••

Fossils of zebra ancestors were discovered in China and Uzbekistan, suggesting that they lived in Asia over two million years ago.

Zebra in Kenya.

During the famous Serengeti Migration, over 75,000 zebras migrate from northern Tanzania to the Masai Mara Reserve in Kenya every year. Other, even longer, migrations also take place further south.

• • •

It gets quite dusty where zebras live, but luckily they can close their nostrils to keep the sand out!

• • •

As every zebra's stripes are different, scientists can scan their patterns like bar codes to identify them in the wild. There is even a special software designed for this!

Grévy's zebra.

Plains zebra.

Plains zebras play an essential role in their ecosystem. They are often the first animals to enter an overgrown patch of grassland and munch the old, tough grass nice and short, allowing younger, more tender grass to grow that other grazers, such as Thomson's gazelles and wildebeest, can come in and eat.

• • •

Female zebras are called **mares**, and male zebras are called **stallions**.

• • •

International Zebra Day is celebrated on the 31st of January every year. Its purpose is to raise awareness of conservation efforts for zebras. How will you get involved?

ZEBRA CHARACTERISTICS

Size, features, special traits and more.

Zebras have similar body shapes to horses: thick bodies, thin legs, and a tufted tail.

• • •

The largest zebra is the Grévy's zebra, which weighs 770 to 990 pounds (350 to 450 kilograms). The smallest zebra, the mountain zebra, weighs 529 to 820 lb (204 to 372 kg).

Mountain zebra.

Albino zebra in Kenya.

Zebras vary in height from 1-1.5 m (3.5-5 ft.), foot to shoulder.

• • •

Every zebra has a unique pattern of stripes; no two are the same.

• • •

Although they are rare, albino zebras have been spotted in Mount Kenya. Their stripes are blonde instead of black.

• • •

Zebras are **single-hoofed**. In fact, equids are the only living animal family with one toe.

Scientists don't know for sure why zebras have stripes. There are many theories, including that they confuse predators—especially when in large groups. Lions are colourblind, so it can be confusing when they see a zebra, as everything is in black and white!

• • •

The zebra's short mane stands upright.

• • •

Zebras have teeth that are designed for grazing. Their large incisors are perfect for cutting grass, while their ridged molars do the grinding.

Male zebras have unique spade-shaped teeth that they can use in fighting.

• • •

Zebras' eyes are high up on their heads and to the side, allowing them to keep a lookout over tall grass while they are grazing.

• • •

Zebras' front legs are longer than their back legs, unlike the horse or ass.

• • •

Zebras live for around 20 years in the wild but often live longer in captivity.

Under their coats, zebras' skin is black!

• • •

Some zebras have spots instead of stripes! Although it's rare, several spotted zebras have been seen in the wild—including a black and white polka-dotted plains foal called Tira, born in Kenya's Maasai Mara National Reserve.

• • •

Mountain zebra's hooves are harder and sharper than the other species', which helps them climb up and down the rugged mountain terrain.

Plains zebras in Botswana.

The further south you go in Africa, the fewer stripes plains zebras have on their legs—this can help scientists tell the different subspecies apart. However, they're not sure why this happens.

• • •

The best way to tell the three species of zebras apart is by looking at their butts! So have a look through the pictures in this book and see if you can notice these differences: mountain zebras have a "gridiron" pattern of small stripes above their tail, plains zebras have wider bands across their rears, and Grévy's zebras have a triangle-like pattern on their backsides, along with lots of smaller lines near the tail.

Plains zebras having a drink in Kruger National Park.

ZEBRAS' DAILY LIVES

What do zebras do all day?!

Zebras are grazing **herbivores**, which means they only eat plants. However, they're not too fussy about what they eat and can survive on low-quality food.

• • •

Zebras spend almost all of their day grazing. They're constantly on the move, searching for fresh grass, shrubs and water.

Plains zebras grazing in Tarangire National Park, Tanzania.

Plains zebra herd.

The zebra's main predators in the wild are lions, leopards, cheetahs and hyenas. Although, if they are attacked, they will put up a good fight by biting and kicking.

• • •

A close, stable group of zebras is called a **harem**. A larger group is called a **herd**, and an area that a herd prefers to stay in is called a **territory**.

• • •

A herd of zebras can also be called a **dazzle**!

A dazzle of plains zebras.

Grévy's zebra.

Sometimes several herds of zebras can come together and form **'super herds'**, which consist of thousands of zebras.

• • •

Female zebras in a harem have a very strong bond; they will stick together even if the dominant male dies.

• • •

Although Grévy's zebras are famous for being antisocial, they will form an alliance when faced with a predator.

Zebras will sometimes meet up with other grazing animals, such as antelope and wildebeest, and they all graze and roam together.

When a herd or harem of zebras is approached by a predator, the zebras will form a defiant semi-circle facing them.

This formation helps them look bigger and stronger and hopefully scare off the predator.

· · ·

You can often see mountain and plains zebras grooming each other; this is their way of bonding. Grévy's zebras aren't quite so sociable!

Zebras have several ways of communicating with each other, including a range of sounds, facial expressions and body language. For example, mountain zebras whinny like a horse, plains zebras bark like dogs, and Grévy's zebras make a bray sound like a donkey.

• • •

A happy zebra will sometimes push air between its lips while grazing.

• • •

During the night, at least one harem member will stay awake to keep watch for predators.

You will often see zebras rolling around in dust, water or mud—or twitching their skin; this is to get rid of flies or parasites.

・・・

Zebras spend around 60 per cent of their lives grazing.

・・・

You can't ride a zebra like you can a horse or a donkey because zebras have very different temperaments and can be unpredictable and potentially dangerous.

Zebras can sleep standing up, making them less vulnerable to predators; however, if they want a deep sleep, they need to lie down.

• • •

Zebras are fast! They can run at speeds of up to 40 miles per hour (65 km/h)!

• • •

Although zebras look like peaceful animals, they can be very aggressive if they need to be. Their aggression starts when they transition from being a foal to an adult.

< **Plains zebra on the run.**

Stallions can be very territorial, especially when it comes to females, and have been known to use their fierce kicks and sharp teeth to severely injure and even kill other zebras that get in their way.

• • •

Different species of zebras act differently around other zebras. For example, mountain and plains zebras prefer to live in stable harems, while the Grévy's zebra is more independent and often lives alone.

Plains zebras fighting >

Plains zebra (*E. quagga*)

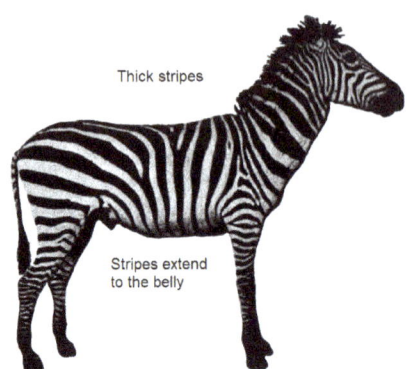

Thick stripes
Stripes extend to the belly

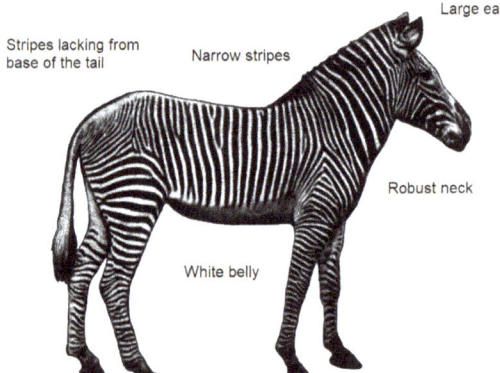

Stripes lacking from base of the tail
Narrow stripes
Large ears
Robust neck
White belly

Grévy's zebra (*E. grevyi*)

Mountain zebra (*E. zebra*)

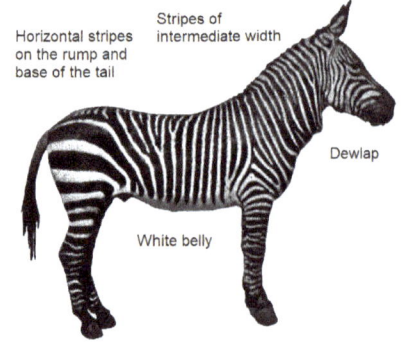

Horizontal stripes on the rump and base of the tail
Stripes of intermediate width
Dewlap
White belly

Zebra Subspecies

There are three living species of zebra: the **Grévy's zebra, the plains zebra,** and the **mountain zebra**. You can use the handy guide on the left to tell them apart.

Zebras have also been cross-bred in captivity with horses, ponies, and donkeys to produce **zebroids, zorses,** and **zonis**.

Let's take a closer look to find out the differences between them!

GRÉVY'S ZEBRA

Equus grevyi

The Grévy's zebra, also known as the **imperial zebra**, is the largest living species in the *Equidae* family (which includes horses and asses). Sadly they are the most threatened species of zebra, and the IUCN lists them as **endangered**.

It is easy to tell the Grévy's zebra apart from the other species by its large ears, narrower stripes, and size. They also don't have any stripes at the base of their tails or on their bellies.

Grévy's zebra live in Ethiopia and Kenya, in semi-arid grasslands where they may go up to five days without water. The Grévy's zebra doesn't live in a harem like the other species. Instead, they often roam around alone, in large scattered groups called territories, and only form close bonds with their foals. There is a dominant stallion in each territory.

The Grévy's zebra was named after King Jules Grévy of France after he was gifted a zebra from the King of Abyssinia in 1882.

PLAINS ZEBRA

Equus quagga

The plains zebra, also known as the **common zebra**, is the least endangered species of zebra. They are widespread and live across most parts of south-eastern Africa. There are six subspecies separated mostly based on where they live. Before the 19th century, there was a seventh subspecies known as the **quagga**. Sadly it was hunted to extinction by European settlers.

Plains zebras are very sociable animals and, like mountain zebras, they live in harems.

Their habitat is usually treeless grassland or savannas ranging from hot tropical to temperate climates.

The plains zebra is medium-sized and has broader stripes than the other species. They are not territorial and migrate between different areas, often depending on the season and access to water.

MOUNTAIN ZEBRA
Equus zebra

The mountain zebra is native to southwestern Africa. They are listed as **vulnerable** by the IUCN, meaning they are at risk of extinction if no conservation efforts are made. However, things are much better than they used to be. In the 1930s, there were only around 100 mountain zebras left in the wild, and they were very close to extinction. Fortunately, conservation programmes have brought population numbers back up.

There are two different subspecies of mountain zebra. One lives in South Africa

(**Cape mountain zebra**), and the other in south-western Angola and Namibia (**Hartmann's mountain zebra**). The mountain zebra is the smallest species of zebra, and its most noticeable feature is its 'dewlap', a flap of skin underneath its neck.

There aren't too many differences between the two subspecies of mountain zebra. However, the ground colour (the area that is not a stripe) is slightly more tan-coloured in the Hartmann's mountain zebra.

Mountain zebras live in a wide range of habitats, but they always prefer hot, rocky, mountainous areas, especially those with lots of grass species to eat. They live in harems, close social groups consisting of one stallion and up to five mares and their offspring.

Cape Mountain Zebra.

FROM BIRTH TO ADULTHOOD

Baby zebras are some of the cutest in the animal world, so let's learn more about their early lives.

Baby zebras are called **foals**.

• • •

As zebras are mammals, their young suckle milk from their mothers.

• • •

The **gestation period** (how long a female is pregnant) for zebras is 11-13 months, depending on the species.

Plains mare with her foal.

Mares usually give birth to one foal at a time, every 2-3 years.

•••

Female plains and mountain zebras, which live in harems, will mate only with the dominant stallion, while Grévy's zebras will attract females into their territories and are much more promiscuous.

•••

When foals are born, their stripes are brown, but they darken as they get older.

It only takes six minutes before a newborn foal can stand up. After 20 minutes, they can walk, and after 40 minutes, they can already run! Their amazingly fast development is important for their survival, as foals are in great danger from predators like lions and coyotes as soon as they're born.

...

When male zebras are between one and three years old, they leave their family groups to form all-male 'bachelor herds' until they're old enough and strong enough to compete for females and become dominant stallions.

Grévy's zebra foal.

Hartmann's mountain zebra foal.

Cape mountain zebra and Hartmann's mountain zebra foals leave their maternal herds at different times. While cape mountain foals move away between 13 and 37 months, Hartmann's mountain foals are usually pushed out of their groups at around 14-16 months.

• • •

When foals are first born, they will follow anything that moves, so the mothers will keep a close watch on them for the first couple of days to make sure they know her scent, sounds and stripe pattern.

Although foals will attempt to start grazing after only a few weeks, they aren't fully weaned off their mother's milk until they are 8-13 months old.

• • •

Foals will follow their mothers and carefully watch what plants they are eating for around one year to know which ones are safe. They will also learn the migration routes and how to protect themselves from predators before heading off on their own.

• • •

Foals can recognise their mothers by their stripes, which is called imprinting.

It's a tough life for zebra foals, and sadly, only 50 per cent of foals make it to adulthood.

• • •

In plains and mountain zebras, the entire harem will protect the foals if a threat comes their way. However, Grévy's zebra mares will form small groups and put their foals into a 'kindergarten', guarded by a territorial male while they go for water or food.

• • •

Male Grévy's zebras will often take care of a foal that isn't their own, whereas plain and mountain zebras don't tolerate foals that aren't theirs in their herd.

ZEBRAS IN POPULAR CULTURE

Real, animated, modern and ancient—zebras have played an important role in society for thousands of years.

Zebra is pronounced differently in British and American English.

American English is pronounced with a long first vowel (*zee*-bra), while the British use a short vowel (ze-bra).

Image copyright Ferrara.

Yipes the Zebra has been the mascot of *Fruit Stripe Gum* for over two decades—he has outlived their other mascots and features prominently on their packaging and advertising.

• • •

Zebras have featured in African art and culture for thousands of years. For example, there are rock paintings of zebras in southern Africa that date back over 28,000 years!

Plains zebra mare and foal.

There are many folk tales about how zebras got their stripes. For example, the San people of Namibia tell the story of how the zebra got scorched in a fire after getting into a fight with a baboon and from then on it had stripes.

• • •

"A man without culture is like a zebra without stripes" is a common Massai (an ethnic group from parts of Kenya and Tanzania) saying that is commonly used worldwide.

The plains zebra is the national animal of Botswana.

• • •

There are many great movies that feature animated zebras, including *Khumba*, *The Lion King*, *Racing Stripes* and *Madagascar*. So which ones have you seen?

• • •

The TV show *Zou* on Disney+ (Universal Kids in the USA) follows the adventures of a young fictional zebra called Zou.

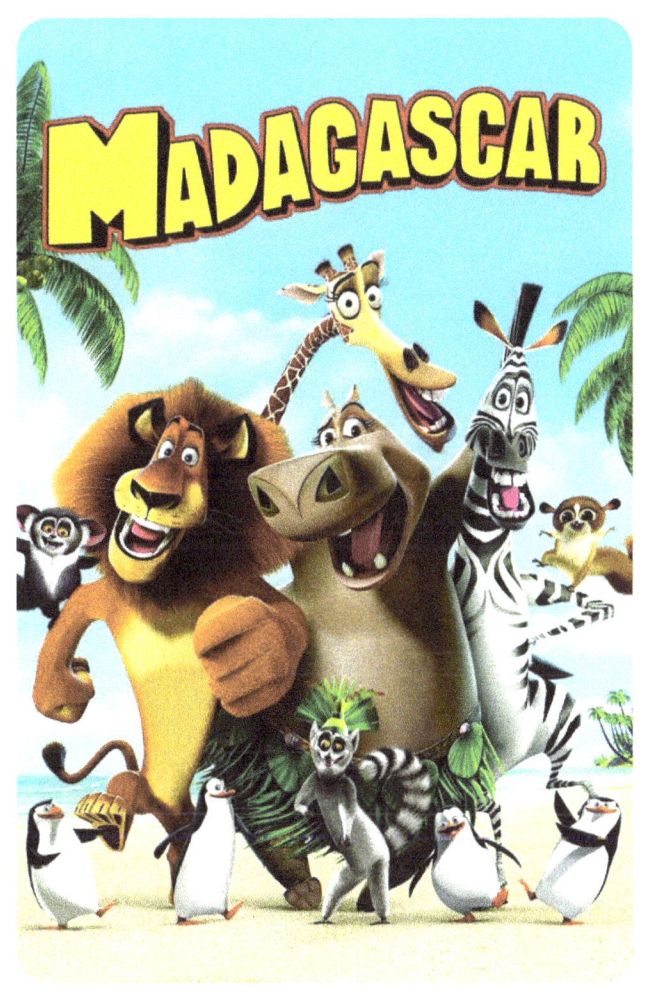

Madagascar **movie poster. Can you spot Marty the zebra?** Copyright: *Dreamworks*.

Many famous artists have been inspired by zebras for their paintings, including Christopher Wood, Lucian Freud and Sidney Nolan.

• • •

Zebras are a popular exhibit at zoos around the world. Since the Roman Empire, they have been kept in captivity and were often given as gifts between royalty and aristocrats.

< **Christopher Wood's painting, "Zebra and Parachute", painted in 1930.**

In 1762 Queen Charlotte of England received a zebra as a wedding gift. It lived in the garden at Buckingham Palace, where thousands of fascinated British people would come to see it.

• • •

The first-ever zebra crossing was installed in Slough, the United Kingdom, in 1951. Now it is one of the world's most used methods for road safety.

One of the most famous zebra crossings in the world is at Abbey Road, London.   >

ZEBRAS: CONSERVATION

Unfortunately, two out of three zebra species are in danger of extinction.

There are only around 2,000 Grévy's zebras left in the wild, a 54 per cent decline since the 1980s. The **IUCN** says that Grévy's zebras have *"undergone one of the most substantial reductions of range of any African mammal."*

Plains zebras are listed as **vulnerable**, with only 9000 left in the wild. Mountain zebras, although numbers are now increasing, are still listed as **near-threatened**.

The biggest threat to zebras is humans. Hunting and habitat destruction via farming are the main problems. However, droughts and other extreme weather conditions also play a part.

While this is sad news, there is still hope. Around the world, conservation programmes are working hard to take care of zebras, both in the wild and in captivity. Zebras are a common sight in zoos worldwide, and they do well living in captivity. They will usually live 5-10 years longer than in the wild when treated well.

Some organisations that focus on zebra conservation include the African Wildlife Foundation, Grevy's Zebra Trust and the WWF. You can visit their websites or social media to find out ways that you can get involved, including adopting or sponsoring a zebra.

ZEBRA *quiz*

Now test your knowledge in our Zebra Quiz! Answers are on page 80.

1 On which continent do zebras live?

2 What are male and female zebras called?

3 On what day is International Zebra Day celebrated?

4 Can you name the three species of zebra?

5 What is another name for the plains zebra?

6 Which zebra species is the largest?

7 Can you name the two subspecies of mountain zebra?

8 Zebras front legs are longer than their back legs. True or false?

9 What colour is the zebra's skin?

10 Which zebra species has sharper and harder hooves than the others?

11 Zebras like to eat insects. True or false?

12 What is another name for a herd of zebras?

13 Zebras can sleep standing up. True or false?

14 How fast can zebras run?

15 What is the gestation period of zebras?

16 What colour are a foal's stripes when it's born?

17 How long does it take before a foal can run?

18 Which African country has the plains zebra as its national animal?

19 Where was the first-ever zebra crossing installed?

20 Which species of zebra is most at risk of extinction?

ANSWERS:

1. Africa.
2. Males are called stallions, females are called mares.
3. 31st January.
4. Grévy's, plains and mountain.
5. The common zebra.
6. Grévy's zebra.
7. Cape mountain zebra and Hartmann's mountain zebra.
8. True.
9. Black.
10. Mountain zebras.
11. False. They are herbivores, meaning they only eat plants.
12. A dazzle.
13. True.
14. Up to 40 miles per hour (65 km/h).
15. 11-13 months.
16. Brown.
17. 40 minutes.
18. Botswana.
19. Slough, United Kingdom.
20. Grévy's zebra.

Zebra WORD SEARCH

```
D S T A L L I O N S Z R
F W G F D S X V N T G E
V T E N D A N G E R E D
N R A B R F S F J I V A
R E R E W R A S D P U Z
E H E R B I V O R E Y Z
S V X G Z C D E W S E L
K Z E B R A T E Z C W E
J D Q P F E V F D S J D
D B A H E N V T R E V A
F V Z W F O E Y D C E C
B X F P L A I N S B S X
```

Can you find all the words below in the word search puzzle on the left?

ZEBRA	**GREVYS**	**STALLION**
AFRICA	**STRIPES**	**DAZZLE**
HERBIVORE	**ENDANGERED**	**PLAINS**

THE ULTIMATE ZEBRA BOOK

WORD SEARCH SOLUTION

D	S	T	A	L	L	I	O	N	S	Z	R
F	W	G	F	D	S	X	V	N	T	G	E
V	T	E	N	D	A	N	G	E	R	E	D
N	R	A	B	R	F	S	F	J	I	V	A
R	E	R	E	W	R	A	S	D	P	U	Z
E	H	E	R	B	I	V	O	R	E	Y	Z
S	V	X	G	Z	C	D	E	W	S	E	L
K	Z	E	B	R	A	T	E	Z	C	W	E
J	D	Q	P	F	E	V	F	D	S	J	D
D	B	A	H	E	N	V	T	R	E	V	A
F	V	Z	W	F	O	E	Y	D	C	E	C
B	X	F	P	L	A	I	N	S	B	S	X

SOURCES

Zebra - Wikipedia (2022). Available at: https://en.wikipedia.org/wiki/Zebra (Accessed: 14 April 2022).

Mountain zebra - Wikipedia (2022). Available at: https://en.wikipedia.org/wiki/Mountain_zebra (Accessed: 14 April 2022).

Only, A. (2022) Sophie's Top Ten Interesting Zebra Facts, Sophie Allport®. Available at: https://www.sophieallport.com/blogs/lifestyle/our-top-ten-interesting-zebra-facts (Accessed: 14 April 2022).

Zebra facts for kids | National Geographic Kids (2017). Available at: https://www.natgeokids.com/uk/discover/animals/general-animals/zebra-facts/ (Accessed: 14 April 2022).

Magazine, S. and Daley, J. (2017) Why Horses and Their Ilk Are the Only One-Toed Animals Still Standing, Smithsonian Magazine. Available at: https://www.smithsonianmag.com/smart-news/study-shows-how-horses-ended-only-one-toe-180964618/ (Accessed: 14 April 2022).

Equus zebra (mountain zebra) (2022). Available at: https://animaldiversity.org/accounts/Equus_zebra/ (Accessed: 14 April 2022).

Zebra Facts (2014). Available at: https://www.livescience.com/27443-zebras.html (Accessed: 14 April 2022).

10 Fascinating Facts About Zebras (2022). Available at: https://www.treehugger.com/things-you-didnt-know-about-zebras-4864185 (Accessed: 15 April 2022).

Rare polka-dotted zebra foal photographed in Kenya (2022). Available at: https://www.nationalgeographic.com/animals/article/zebra-pseudo-melanism-kenya-masai (Accessed: 15 April 2022).

Zebra Fact Sheet | Blog | Nature | PBS (2020). Available at: https://www.pbs.org/wnet/nature/blog/zebra-fact-sheet/ (Accessed: 18 April 2022).

7 Facts to Celebrate International Zebra Day! (2019). Available at: https://nationalzoo.si.edu/animals/news/7-facts-celebrate-international-zebra-day (Accessed: 18 April 2022).

How Does an Antelope Take Care of Its Young? (2022). Available at: https://animals.mom.com/antelope-care-its-young-8836.html (Accessed: 18 April 2022).

And that's all, folks!

We'd love it if you left us a **review**—they always make us smile, but more importantly they help other readers make better buying decisions.

Visit us at

www.bellanovabooks.com

for more fun fact books and giveaways!

ALSO BY JENNY KELLETT

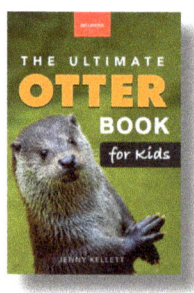  

... and more!

Available at

www.bellanovabooks.com

and all major online bookstores.

www.ingramcontent.com/pod-product-compliance
Lightning Source LLC
LaVergne TN
LVHW050134080526
838202LV00061B/6487